This book belongs to:

....

My FIRST Bible Stories

Written by Rachel Moss and Catherine Allison
Cover illustrated by Emily Dove
Illustrated by Iris Deppe, John Joven, Xuan Le, Tiziana Longo,
Madison Mastrangelo, Laura Rigo, and Luisa Uribe

Every effort has been made to acknowledge the contributors to this book.
If we have made any errors, we will be pleased to rectify them in future editions.

First published 2016 Parragon Books, Ltd.

ISBN: 978-1-68052-459-8

Parragon Books is an imprint of Cottage Door Press, LLC.
Parragon Books® and the Parragon® logo are
registered trademarks of Cottage Door Press, LLC.

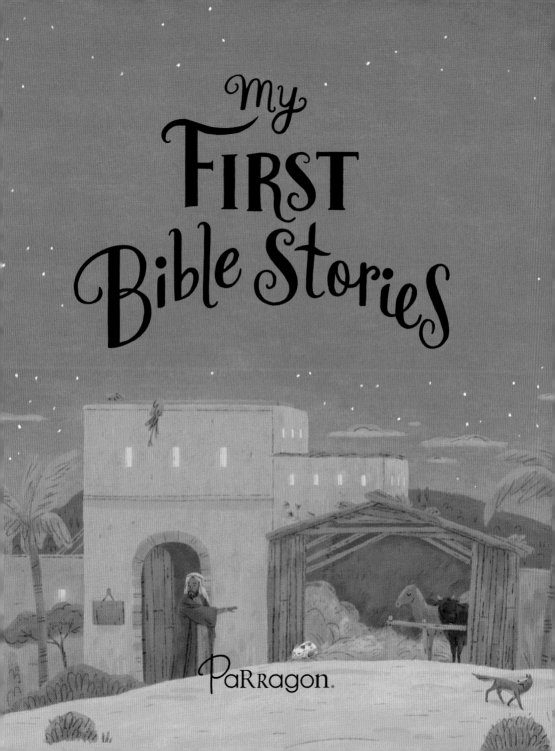

My FIRST Bible Stories

PaRragon.

Contents

The Old Testament

The New Testament

The Creation Story

In the beginning, before time began, there was nothing. Nothing to see. Nothing to hear. Nothing to touch or smell. There was only silence. God moved alone through the inky darkness.

Then God created the heavens and the Earth, and the Earth was covered by water.

"Let there be light," God said.

It was faint at first, a flicker in the darkness that grew and grew. It became a glowing ball that pushed the gloom aside, soft and yellow, then red, pink, and dazzling gold.

God delighted in its loveliness. The changing light seemed to have a life of its own, and God called it "day." When the light faded into darkness, He named it "night."

It was the very first day of the world.

On the second day, when the light came back, God made the sky. It was a soft, bright blue, and it hung over the Earth like a canopy.

On the third day of the world, God drew back the choppy waters, so that solid ground appeared. The great pools of water, blue like the sky and shimmering in the light, He named "seas." He called the big, muddy areas of ground "land."

The land was flat and bare, so God shaped it into mountains, plains, and deep valleys. Under His guiding hand, greenery covered the Earth. Grasses and plants of every size, shape, and color took root; sweet-smelling flowers blossomed; sticky buds opened; and vines coiled upward.

Trees sprang from the ground, their branches reaching for the sky, growing tall and heavy with fruit. The Earth had become lush and green, and brimmed with plant life.

On the fourth day, God said, "Let there be signs to mark the day and night."

He made the fiery Sun to show the day and the gentle Moon to shine at night. During the day, the Moon hid in the shadows. At night, the Sun turned its golden face away, while the Moon cast its silvery beams over the land.

God also brightened the night sky with millions upon millions of tiny glittering stars. He felt pleased with the beautiful world He had created.

God's new world was a peaceful land filled with flowers, trees, and rushing rivers, but there were no birds to perch in the trees. There were no bees to buzz from flower to flower, nor fish to leap through the waves. The only sounds were the whisper of the wind among the leaves and the waves lapping the shores.

On the fifth day, God filled the waters with living creatures. Suddenly, the sea teemed with fish that moved as one. He made whales that sent great plumes of spray high up into the sky, and dolphins that leaped playfully in and out of the waves.

He made jellyfish that shimmered like
moonlight, shellfish that sparkled like
precious stones, and tiny crabs that waved
their claws on the golden sands.

Then God said, "Let there be creatures of the air that will fill the sky with life."

There began a great fluttering of feathers and flapping of wings, and a cloud of birds and insects of all shapes and sizes rose into the sky. Tiny chirruping sparrows mingled with colorful parakeets and silent, gliding hawks. The sky was alive with color and sound as the twittering birds found shelter among the trees and bushes, discovered fruit, and washed their feathers in the bright streams. Their happy songs filled God's ears, and He blessed them.

On the sixth day of the world, God said, "Now, let there be creatures on the land!" and the Earth began to shake with the thunder of a thousand feet.

The world hummed with voices large and small, jostling to be heard. Regal lions prowled beside mighty elephants and rhinos. Monkeys swung through the trees, cackling to each other, and bears lumbered through the undergrowth.

Fierce animals paced side by side with the gentlest of God's creatures. Everyone, from the tiny shrews to the tall giraffes, was looking for a new home. Some liked the cool of the snowy mountains, and some preferred the heat of the rain forests. Snakes slithered into the jungles, crocodiles hid in rivers, and squirrels climbed tall trees. The world pulsed with life.

God looked around and was happy with what He saw.
But something was missing.

"Who will care for all the animals?" God asked Himself.

He took handfuls of earth and shaped a creature who looked like Him. He breathed life into him and called him "man." Then he took a rib from the man. With the rib, God created "woman." The man and woman opened their eyes and stared around them in wonder. Slowly, they stretched their arms and legs, and rose to their feet. They stood in front of God, holding hands, as beautiful and innocent as the new world.

God blessed them, and named the man Adam and the woman Eve.

"Your job is to look after the wonders I have created," He said. "You will rule over the fish in the sea, the birds in the sky, and every creature on the Earth. You will have fruit to eat and water to drink. I want you to enjoy your life here."

God's work was done. The world was every bit as beautiful as He had imagined.

It was the seventh day, and God rested.

Next, God made a beautiful garden for Adam and Eve, and named it Eden. There were flowers, and trees full of delicious fruit to eat, and velvet-soft grass to lie on. A sparkling stream gave Adam and Eve clean water to drink.

There was a huge tree in the middle of the garden. Its branches reached into the sky like upstretched arms, and God named it the Tree of Knowledge.

"You can pick fruit from any tree in the garden, except the Tree of Knowledge," He told Adam and Eve. "If you eat from that tree, you will die."

Adam and Eve listened to everything God told them. They had all that they needed and they were happy. They cared for the animals and the garden, just as God had told them.

One day, Eve was picking berries near the Tree of Knowledge when she heard rustling in the leaves of the tree. A snake was watching her, its tongue flicking in and out.

"Sssmell the sssweet fruit," the snake hissed. "Try it. Tassste it!"

"No," Eve replied. "God has told us we must not eat the fruit from the Tree of Knowledge or we will die."

The snake shook its head. "It would make you as wissse as God," it said. "Jussst one bite would make you a goddessss."

The snake's words made
Eve long to try it. Slowly,
she plucked a ripe fruit and
drew it toward her. It smelled
sweet and delicious. Her
heart thumped with fear
and excitement.

Eve could not resist. She took a tiny bite of the fruit. Adam saw her and, although he knew that it was wrong, he burned with curiosity. So Eve handed him the fruit and he tried it. Smiling, the snake slithered away.

God knew at once what Adam and Eve had done. He was upset and angry.

"You must leave Eden," He told them. "From now on, the lives of humankind will be full of trouble and worry. Now that you have eaten from the Tree of Knowledge, your bodies will eventually die. But I will find a way to save you."

Adam and Eve shivered and wept as they left Eden behind them. Greed had taken them from a place of gentle breezes to a cruel world where the wind bit and the rain soaked their bodies.

But God, who loves His people, gave Adam and Eve something very special. He gave them hope. Perhaps one day, He told them, humankind might yet return to the beautiful garden of Eden and to the love of God.

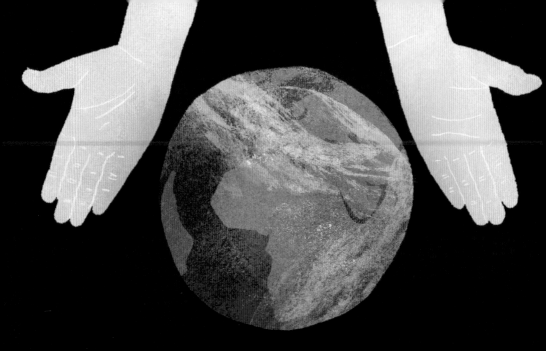

Noah's Ark

Long, long ago, when the world was still new, God saw that all was not well. Golden sun still warmed the days on Earth, silver moonlight gilded the nights, and the hills, valleys, rivers, and seas were as beautiful as on the day God made them. But the world had changed. The people had become wicked. They fought one another, hurt one another, and made mischief. They had forgotten that God wanted them to be good—in fact, they had forgotten God completely. Seeing this made God so unhappy that He wished He'd never made people. He decided that something must be done.

As God looked down on the world, His eyes fell upon one man, whose name was Noah. Noah was the only man on Earth who remembered God. He worked hard every day, despite the fact that he was very old. His wife, his three sons, and his sons' wives all worked hard, too. They were happy, kind to each other, and good to their neighbors, even though they received no kindness in return. They lived a good life—the sort of life God had hoped all people would live when He created them.

God was pleased with Noah and his family. He decided that they deserved to live on Earth and He would protect them. But everyone else had been wicked, and they could not be saved.

God told Noah about His plan
to change the world.

"The world is full of wickedness,"
God said, "so I am going to send
a great flood to wash it
clean. Nearly everyone and
everything will be wiped away,
apart from you and your
family, Noah. The world
will begin again, as fresh and
good as when it was first created,
and you and your family will
live there."

Noah was very frightened.

"What must I do?" he
asked, trembling.

"You should build an ark," said
God. "It must be big enough to hold
two of every animal in the world—one male
and one female—and food for all of them.
It must be strong and watertight, because
it will be battered by the flood waters
for many days."

"I will do exactly as you say,"
said Noah.

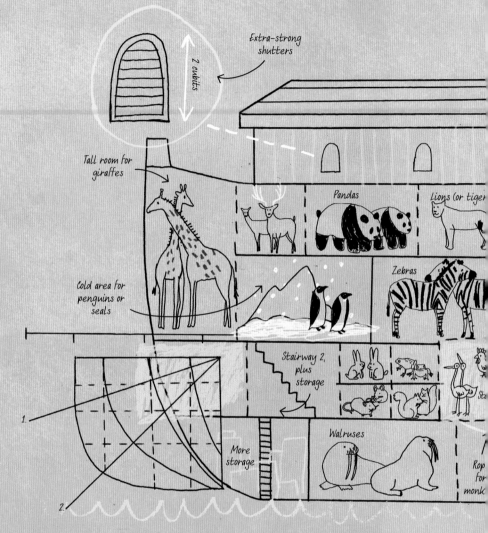

Extra-strong shutters

2 cubits

Tall room for giraffes

Cold area for penguins or seals

Pandas

Lions (or tiger

Zebras

Stairway 2, plus storage

More storage

Walruses

Rop
for
monk

Sto

1.

2.

Noah was glad that he and his family would be saved from the flood, but he was sad about what would happen to the world and all the other people, and worried about what God had told him to do.

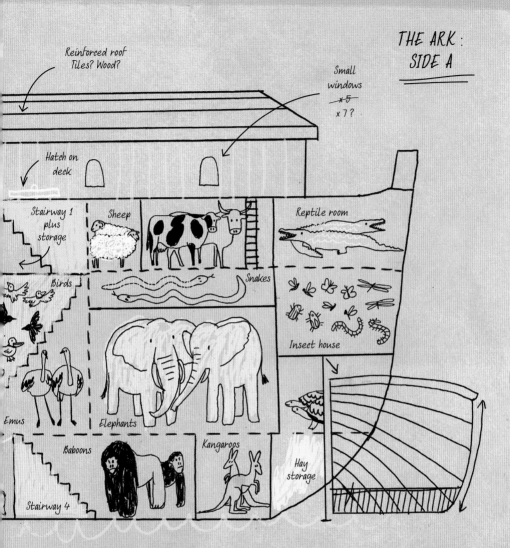

Reinforced roof
Tiles? Wood?

Small
windows
x 5
x 7 ?

Hatch on
deck

Stairway 1
plus
storage

Sheep

Reptile room

Birds

Snakes

Insect house

Emus

Elephants

Baboons

Kangaroos

Hay
storage

Stairway 4

"How can I build such an ark? I'm not a shipbuilder,"
he thought. "And how can I collect so many animals? God
expects so much of me and I'm afraid I will fail."

But God wouldn't let Noah fail. He was there beside Noah
every step of the way, helping him and telling him what to do.

Noah and his sons worked hard, chopping, sawing, sanding, and hammering, and gradually the ark took shape.

While Noah worked, God spoke to him.

"It will rain for forty days and forty nights, and the land will be covered with water. But you, Noah, will be safe in the ark."

As Noah and his sons worked, their neighbors watched from a distance.

"What are you doing, Noah?" they asked, laughing at him. "Why do you need a boat when the sea is miles away?"

Noah heard them laughing, but he took no notice.

After many weeks, the ark was finished. It was taller, longer, and stronger than any boat there had ever been. It was slick, smooth, and shiny on the outside, with strong shutters at the windows and heavy locks on the door—the perfect boat for stormy weather. Inside, there were many rooms, some wide enough for the largest pair of elephants to walk side by side, others high enough for the tallest giraffes to stand in without bending their necks.

All of a sudden, dark clouds appeared in the sky and thunder rumbled. The people who had been laughing at Noah saw that the weather was changing and started to head for home.

"Perhaps Noah isn't such a fool after all," said one.
"There's a storm coming for sure, and he'll be safe and

Noah began to gather the animals—a male and a female of every creature that hopped, walked, crawled, or flew on Earth. There were cats, bats, and rats, monkeys and donkeys, hooting owls and wolves that howled, big baboons and little raccoons—so many animals, of all shapes and sizes. Noah and his sons led the animals up the gangplank and into the ark as the rain began to fall.

"We don't have much time," thought Noah.

The sky turned black and the rain fell harder. Noah's wife, his sons, and his sons' wives made sure all the animals were safely on board, then they went into the ark. With one last glance at the world he loved, Noah went inside, too, and shut the heavy door behind him.

Outside the ark, rain fell everywhere. Not a soft drizzle, but soak-to-the-skin, drench-to-the-bone rain. Raindrops became puddles, and puddles flowed into streams, oozed into lakes, and poured into wild rivers. Then all the rivers joined together and became an angry ocean. The once-dry land was overwhelmed, and hills and homes were gone forever.

Noah and the animals watched through the windows, safe and dry inside their ark.

For forty days and forty nights, it rained. The ark was pulled and pushed, up and down, to and fro on the rainwater ocean. Inside, the animals were frightened and Noah did his best to calm them. He trusted God and knew that all would be well in the end.

At long last, the rain stopped, just as God had said it would, and the ark lay still on the water. Then, strong winds began to blow. Little by little, the water level dropped and the tips of the mountains appeared. The ark came to rest on one of them—a mountain called Ararat. It seemed that the ark's journey was over.

Noah watched from a window, as land continued to appear. Then he sent a raven out into the world to see what it could find. An hour later, it came back tired and worn—and Noah knew there was nowhere for it to land.

A week later, Noah sent out a dove. After some hours, it returned with an olive twig in its beak—and Noah knew it had found at least one tree with branches above the water. It meant that Earth was drying out.

"Not long to wait now," he thought.

After one more week, Noah sent out the dove again. This time, the bird did not return—and Noah knew it had found a dry place to land.

"Now it is safe to leave the ark," he said to his family.

Noah flung open the doors, and the animals filed out of the ark. They raced away in all directions, glad to stretch their legs and run free. The birds flew off to find twigs to build new nests, and the deer trotted off to search for fresh, green grass to eat. The giraffes walked and the lions ran, the monkeys scampered, and the kangaroos hopped. Soon, they would all find new homes and raise their families on the new, dry land.

After all the animals had left the ark, Noah and his family left, too. Noah wanted to thank God, so he built an altar of stones and bowed his head to pray.

"You saved me from the flood and brought me to dry land again," said Noah. "I will always be thankful."

God heard Noah's prayer and was pleased.

"Now is the time for a new beginning on Earth," He said.
"I bless you and your family, and I wish you well. You must
have lots of children, so the world will be filled with people
again. All Earth's riches are yours—the animals and plants,
the land, and the seas. They belong to you, and you must take
care of them."

"Thank you, God," said Noah.

"One more thing," God continued. "I promise that I will never send another flood to destroy the world. Look up and you will see a sign."

Noah looked up at the sky. The gray storm clouds drifted away and bright rays of sunlight shone for the first time since before the flood. As Noah watched, God made a brilliant rainbow appear, which stretched from one end of Earth to the other.

Then, God spoke again.

"Whenever you see a rainbow in the sky, you will remember this day and my promise to you. Now, Noah, go and begin your new life."

Full of joy and thankfulness, Noah walked down the mountain to join his family and the new beautiful world.

Now, when we see a rainbow in the sky, we remember God's promise to Noah. It's also a promise from God to us and to our beautiful world.

The Tower of Babel

Time went by, and Noah's family began to fill the world, just as God had wanted. There were grandchildren, great-grandchildren, and great-great-grandchildren.

Some of the family traveled to a place called Babylonia. They learned how to make bricks and built homes for themselves. They thought they were very clever.

One day, someone suggested that the Babylonians should build the tallest tower in the whole world, so that everyone would know how clever they were. It would be named the Tower of Babel. They quickly set to work.

God watched as the people built the tower. He watched the walls grow higher and higher, and it made Him very sad. He knew the people were not thinking about Him—they were thinking only about their own importance. Soon, they would become as wicked as the people had been before the great flood.

God knew the people had to be able to talk to each other in order to build the tower. If they spoke in different languages, they wouldn't understand one another, and the building would have to stop. So God made all His people speak in different languages and sent them to live in other countries around the world. The people couldn't work together, and the tall Tower of Babel remained unfinished forever.

Abraham and Sarah

One of Noah's descendants was a man named Abraham. He was a good person who believed in God.

One day, God told Abraham to leave his home. Abraham trusted God, so he and his wife Sarah did as God said.

Their journey to find a new home took several months. Then God spoke to Abraham again.

"Look about you," He said. "All the land you can see will be yours forever. You will have as many children as there are stars in the sky. You will be the father of a great nation."

"How can that be?" asked Abraham. "My wife and I are too old to have children."

"Trust me," said God. "You will have a son."

A few years later, three strangers came to Abraham's house and he welcomed them inside.

"We have wonderful news for you," said the strangers. "In nine months' time, Sarah will have a baby son."

Nine months later, Sarah gave birth to a baby boy, named Isaac.

"God also promised that my family will become a great nation," thought Abraham, "and I know He always keeps His promises."

Sure enough, that is exactly what happened.

Jacob and Esau

Abraham's son Isaac grew up and married a woman named Rebekah. After they had been married for a while, Rebekah had twin boys, Esau and Jacob. Esau was Isaac's favorite child, but Rebekah loved Jacob more.

The twins grew up to be very different—they didn't even look alike! Jacob had smooth skin, but Esau's skin was hairy.

As Isaac grew old, he went blind. He knew he would die soon and wanted to bless Esau as the new head of the family, since he was the older twin. But Rebekah wanted Jacob to receive Isaac's blessing, so she made a plan. While Esau was out, Rebekah dressed Jacob in Esau's clothes. She covered his arms with goatskin, to make them seem hairy like his brother's. Then she sent him to Isaac.

When Isaac touched his son's hairy arm, he believed that it was Esau's, but the voice sounded wrong.

"Are you really Esau?" Isaac asked his son.

"Yes, I am Esau," Jacob lied to his father.

So Isaac gave his blessing to Jacob instead of Esau.

Esau was very angry when he found out what Jacob had done. In fact, Jacob was afraid his brother might kill him, so he ran away to stay with relatives.

Jacob had lied, and he had cheated his brother, but God didn't leave him. He had plans for Jacob, so He forgave him and helped him. One night, God came to Jacob in a dream. Jacob saw a staircase reaching up to heaven, with angels moving up and down it.

"I am the God of Abraham and Isaac," God said, "and I will make this land your home. I will bless you, your children, and your children's children. I will watch over you wherever you go, and I will bring you back home."

"If You protect me and bring me safely back home as You have said," Jacob prayed, "then You will always be my God."

In time, Jacob married and traveled home to Canaan. He was afraid that Esau was still angry with him, so he prayed to God that he and his brother would be friends. God heard his prayer, and Esau welcomed Jacob back home with open arms.

Jacob had twelve sons and, in time, they grew into a great nation. Many years later, the family came to be known as the "Children of Israel" or "Hebrews." God had kept His promise.

Joseph and His Coat of Many Colors

Of Jacob's twelve sons, Joseph was his favorite. Joseph was kind and helpful, and his mother Rachel had been Jacob's most beloved wife. She had died, and Jacob missed her very much, but Joseph reminded him of her every day.

Jacob's ten eldest sons were too busy to spend much time with him, and his youngest son Benjamin was too young, but Joseph, the second youngest, loved sitting and talking with his father. They were good friends as well as being father and son.

Jacob enjoyed showing Joseph how much he was loved. He bought him a special coat, woven in bright, beautiful colors, to keep him warm while he and his older brothers tended the sheep on the hills.

"Thank you, Father," said Joseph, hugging Jacob. "I love it!"

Joseph's brothers felt jealous, because Joseph was their
father's favorite. They had only plain, threadbare jackets,
so when they saw Joseph's new coat, they disliked him
even more.

One day, the brothers were walking home from the hills to help harvest the fields in Canaan, where they lived. Joseph's brothers were ignoring him and muttering mean things about him. But Joseph didn't notice that they were being unkind, because he was thinking about a dream he had had the night before.

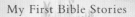

"I had a dream about the harvest last night," he said. "We each had a sheaf of golden corn standing in the field. Mine stood tall, while your smaller sheaves bowed down to it. I think it's a message from God. What do you think it means?"

His brothers were furious.

"Do you think you're better than us?" they asked.

Joseph felt terrible. He wanted his brothers to love him, but telling them about his dream had made them hate him even more.

A short time later, Joseph had another dream that he couldn't understand. He decided to tell his father and his brothers about it when they were all together at home. Perhaps his father would know what it meant.

"I had another dream last night," Joseph said one evening, trying to ignore the angry looks from his brothers. "This time, the Sun and Moon and eleven stars in the glittering night sky were bowing down to me. What could it mean?"

His brothers were enraged, and even his father frowned.

"Do you think that your brothers and I will come and bow down to you?" Jacob asked.

Joseph didn't dare to say any more, and Jacob didn't mention it again, but he didn't forget about Joseph's strange dream.

Over time, Joseph's brothers grew more and more jealous of Joseph. They left him out of everything and wanted to make him suffer for being their father's favorite.

One day, when the older brothers were out looking after the sheep and Benjamin was at home, Jacob sent Joseph to find out how they were doing. When the older brothers saw Joseph coming in his colorful coat, all their hateful feelings bubbled up.

"I've had enough of this dreamer," one brother snarled.

"If only we could get rid of him," said another.

"We could do what we liked to him out here," said a third. "We could say it was a wild animal. He might even die."

The others felt such hatred toward Joseph that hurting him suddenly didn't seem like such a bad thing to do. Only Reuben, Joseph's eldest brother, tried to stop them.

"Let's not kill him. Just throw him into a dry well," he said, thinking that he could rescue Joseph later when the others had calmed down.

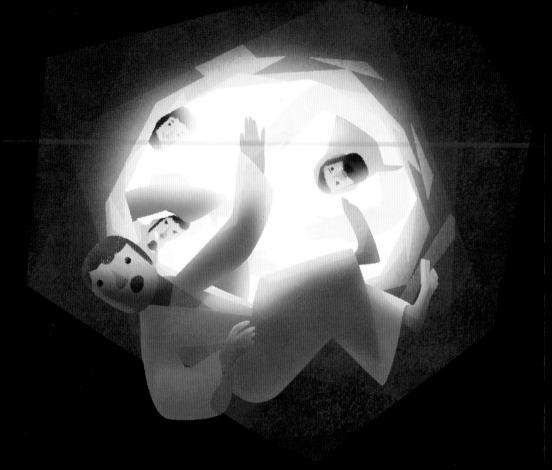

The other brothers ripped Joseph's beautiful coat from his back and threw him into a dry well. But, while Reuben was tending to the sheep, they saw a group of travelers, called Ishmaelites, coming their way.

Another brother, Judah, had an idea. "We won't gain anything from killing Joseph," he said. "Let's sell him!"

So the greedy brothers sold Joseph for twenty pieces of silver. Shocked and hurt, Joseph was carried far away.

Joseph and His Coat of Many Colors

Reuben was horrified when he found out what his brothers had done. "How can we explain this to our father?" he cried.

"We'll make it sound like an accident," said Judah.

The brothers dipped Joseph's coat in animal blood, so it looked as if a wild beast had eaten him. Then, they took it home to Jacob. Believing that his dearest son was dead, Jacob's heart broke into pieces.

"I will go to my grave mourning for my son," he said.

Joseph was taken far away to Egypt. He was sold as a slave to a man named Potiphar. Potiphar was an important man who worked for Pharaoh, who was in charge of all Egypt.

"I am now a slave," Joseph said to himself. "It must be God's plan for me."

At first, Joseph's life in Egypt was not too bad. Joseph knew that God would want him to do his best. He worked hard and soon became an important servant. God blessed Potiphar's house, because Joseph was there.

His master Potiphar trusted him and everyone liked him—everyone except Potiphar's wife. Filled with wickedness and jealousy, she told Potiphar lies about Joseph to get him into trouble. Poor Joseph was thrown into prison.

But Joseph did not feel alone in prison, because God stayed with him. He made friends among the other prisoners, too.

One day, Joseph heard two other prisoners talking in worried voices. They were Pharaoh's butler and baker, and they had each had a strange dream on the same night.

"I understand a little about dreams," he said. "May I try to help?"

"I dreamed I saw a vine with three branches heavy with ripe grapes," the butler said. "I squeezed the juice from the grapes into Pharaoh's cup."

"That's simple," said Joseph. "In three days, Pharaoh will set you free."

Next, the baker told Joseph his dream.

"I had three baskets of bread for Pharaoh," he said. "But birds swooped out of the sky and ate them all."

"I'm sorry," said Joseph, his heart aching for the man. "In three days, Pharaoh will have you killed."

Everything that Joseph said came true.

Two years later, Pharaoh dreamed that seven fat cows came out of the River Nile. After them came seven thin and bony cows, which ate up the fat cows.

The same night, Pharaoh dreamed of seven healthy ears of corn. Another seven ears of corn sprouted, tiny and shriveled, and swallowed up the healthy corn.

"Who can tell me what these dreams mean?" cried Pharaoh.

Pharaoh's butler suddenly remembered the man in prison.

Pharaoh sent for Joseph and described his dreams to him.

"God is sending you a message," Joseph explained. "Seven years of good harvests are coming, followed by seven years of terrible famine."

Seeing that Joseph was a man of God, Pharaoh freed Joseph and put him in charge of saving Egypt. Joseph became rich and important. He made sure that enough grain was stored up from the good harvests to feed the Egyptian people through the hard years.

Just as Joseph had foreseen, seven years of plenty were followed by terrible famine. People outside of Egypt began to starve. In Canaan, Jacob and his sons were weak and hungry.

"Egypt has plenty of grain," Jacob told his sons. "Surely they can spare some for us."

So the ten eldest sons set off for Egypt, leaving Benjamin at home.

Joseph was in charge of selling grain to people.

When the brothers reached Egypt, they bowed down before Joseph. Not one of them recognized him.

"It's just like my dream," Joseph thought. "At last I understand God's plan."

"We want to buy some grain," the brothers said.

Joseph hoped that his brothers had changed, and thought of a way to find out. "I think you're spies," he said.

"No, we are all brothers," they cried. "Once there were twelve of us, but one is dead. Our youngest brother is with our father Jacob, in Canaan."

"Bring your youngest brother to me, to prove that your story is true," Joseph said. "Otherwise, I will have you all killed."

He sent the brothers home with sacks of food. But he kept his brother Simeon in Egypt, to make sure that the others would return.

"This is God's punishment for the way we treated Joseph," the brothers whispered to each other.

Tears came to Joseph's eyes when he saw the fear on their faces.

At first, Jacob refused to let Benjamin go to Egypt. Since he had lost Joseph, Benjamin had become Jacob's favorite son, and he didn't want to lose him, even if it meant Simeon would have to stay in Egypt.

But, when they eventually ran out of food, he had to agree.

The brothers returned to Egypt with Benjamin. Joseph released Simeon and invited them all to eat at his house. Then he filled their sacks with food, refusing to accept their money. Secretly, Joseph asked a servant to hide a silver cup in Benjamin's sack of food.

Eventually, the brothers got up to leave.

"Stop!" Joseph yelled. "One of you has stolen my silver cup. Guards, search their sacks!"

When the cup was found in Benjamin's sack, the brothers dropped to their knees in front of Joseph.

"Please, imprison one of us instead," they begged. "Losing Benjamin would break our father's heart."

Joseph listened to them plead for Benjamin's life, and knew for certain that they had changed. Tears rolled down his cheeks as he kneeled down beside his brothers.

"Don't you recognize me?" he whispered.

When Joseph's brothers realized who he was, they couldn't speak for shock and shame. But Joseph smiled at them. He knew that this was all part of God's plan.

"I forgive you," he said.

Trembling, his brothers rose and hugged him. Then Joseph asked them to return to Canaan to tell Jacob the good news.

"Bring your families and all your animals back to Egypt," he said. "I will give you the best land here."

When Jacob heard that Joseph was alive, he could hardly believe it. It wasn't until he was standing in front of his beloved son that he knew it was true.

"Father!" cried Joseph, his heart bursting with joy.

They wrapped their arms around each other and wept happy tears. God had brought them back together at last.

Jacob settled comfortably in Egypt, in the region of Goshen, and lived to be a great age.

Moses

After Joseph died, life became very hard for the Israelites in Egypt. There was a new Pharaoh, who was afraid that there were too many of them and that they would turn against the Egyptians, so he made them into slaves. Then Pharaoh ordered that all their baby boys should be killed!

One mother, Jochebed, hid her baby in a basket beside the river—where Pharaoh's daughter found him. Pharaoh's daughter wanted to save the baby's life, so she took him to live with her in the palace. She named him Moses and asked Jochebed to be his nurse. She didn't know that Jochebed was Moses's real mother—it was God's plan that the boy should grow up with his mother beside him. As Moses grew up, his mother secretly told him that he was an Israelite.

One day, Moses attacked a cruel Egyptian master who was beating an Israelite slave. He knew he would be punished by Pharaoh for helping an Israelite, so he ran away to live as a shepherd in the desert.

Many years later, God spoke to Moses.

"I am the God of Abraham, Isaac, and Jacob," He said. "I have seen how My people are suffering, and I want you to go back to Egypt. Tell Pharaoh that he must free the Israelites and let them leave Egypt."

Moses was scared to go back to Egypt, but he could not refuse his God. So he went to Pharaoh and asked him to let the Israelites go. Pharaoh refused.

With that, God decided to punish Pharaoh by sending terrible disasters called plagues to destroy Egypt. The land was attacked by insects and frogs, the crops died, and the people became very sick. Only the Israelites were saved from these plagues.

But proud Pharaoh still would not free the Israelites. So God sent the angel of death to kill the eldest son of every Egyptian family. Pharaoh's son died, too. Only Israelite families were spared.

After this, Pharaoh agreed to let the Israelites go free. But then he changed his mind and sent his soldiers to capture them again! The only way they could escape was across the Red Sea. Moses stretched out his arms and God parted the waters, so that they could cross safely into the desert on the other side. But when the soldiers tried to follow them, God made the water pour down on their heads and every one of them was killed.

The Israelites were free at last! God had kept His promise.

Moses and the Israelites

Thanks to God, the Israelites were free from Egypt, but they were still suffering, because there was no food in the desert. "We would rather have died in Egypt than starve to death here," they moaned. God heard them, and made them a promise.

"I will give you meat every night and bread every day, except on the Sabbath—my day of rest," He said.

That night, a huge flock of birds appeared. They were easy to catch, so the Israelites had plenty of meat to eat.

The next morning, the ground was covered with white, bread-like flakes. They appeared every morning after that and were sweet to eat. The Israelites called them "manna."

Now, the Israelites had food to eat, but no water to drink. The hot sun beat down, and they became thirstier and thirstier.

Moses asked God for help.

"Find a rock at Mount Sinai," said God, "and hit it with your stick."

When Moses did as God had told him, water gushed out of the rock. Now, there was lots of cool, refreshing water for everyone to drink, and the people were happy.

Moses and the Israelites set up camp at the foot of Mount Sinai.

Then, one day, God spoke to them again.

"I have brought you here to be My chosen people," He said. "Will you obey Me?"

"We will," said the Israelites.

"Then I will give you ten special laws, called commandments," said God, "which show you how to serve Me and how to live together."

Two days later, thunder rumbled and lightning flashed at the top of the mountain.

Together, Moses and his brother Aaron climbed the mountain.

When they reached the top, God gave Moses the
Ten Commandments carved on two
stone tablets.

These are God's ten laws:

1. Honor and serve Me alone,
   for I am the only God.
2. Do not make or worship
   any other gods.
3. Treat My name with respect.
4. Keep every Sabbath as a day
   of rest.
5. Respect your father and mother.
6. Do not kill another human being.
7. Husbands and wives must keep
   their love only for each other.
8. Do not steal.
9. Do not tell lies.
10. Do not be greedy for things
    that other people have.

God told Moses how the laws worked, and Moses
explained them to the people. He was God's special
messenger, called a "prophet."

"God loves you," Moses told the people, "and will look
after you as long as you honor Him and obey His laws."

The Israelites Conquer Jericho

The Israelites lived in the desert for forty years. Moses grew old and died, and God chose Joshua to be the new leader.

One day, God said to Joshua, "You must cross the River Jordan into the land I promised you and capture the city of Jericho."

The Israelites traveled to Jericho. The city walls were high and thick with strong gates, and there were soldiers on guard. It looked impossible for the Israelites to capture this city. But God told Joshua exactly what to do.

"Each day, for six days, you must march around the city. Seven priests must go first, blowing their trumpets. On the seventh day, march around the city seven times. Then, the priests must play one long note on their trumpets, and all the people must shout. The walls of Jericho will fall and the city will be yours!"

The Israelites did what God said. Down crashed the walls, and the Israelites captured the city!

This was the first of Joshua's great victories in Canaan. With him as their leader, the Israelites took over the Promised Land—the land that God had promised to Abraham many years before.

The First King of Israel

Many years later, God chose the prophet Samuel to lead the Israelites. Samuel was a fair leader. He loved God and he loved the honest way of life of his people. But the Israelites wanted a king, as other nations had.

Even though Samuel told them that a king might not treat them well, the people insisted. So God told Samuel, "I will give them what they want."

The young man God chose to be king of Israel was named Saul. He was a poor Israelite whose job was to look after his father's donkeys—he had no idea that he was God's chosen king. But Samuel reassured him and told him to trust in God.

In the beginning, Saul was a good ruler, but sadly that did not last. He soon became proud, and thought less about God and more about himself. He was so proud that, when he won battles against Israel's enemies, he thought it was because he was clever, not because God was helping him.

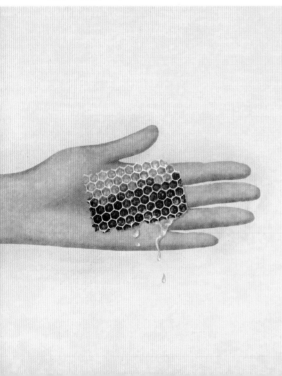

In the middle of one battle, Saul ordered that none of his soldiers should eat until they had won the fight. Anyone who ate would be killed, he said. But Saul's son Jonathan didn't hear the order. He was leading a group of soldiers on the battlefield, and none of them had eaten anything all day. He was hungry, so, when he found a honeycomb, he ate some of the sweet honey. The soldiers with him were shocked at what he had done.

"Didn't you hear the king's command?" they asked. "Anyone who eats before the battle is over must be put to death."

When proud Saul found out that Jonathan had disobeyed him, he would not go back on his word, even to save his own son's life! It was only when the Israelite people stood up to Saul that Jonathan's life was spared.

Even after this, Saul did not change his ways. He did exactly what he wanted, disobeyed God, and would not listen to Samuel. He won more victories—not for God, but to satisfy his own pride and greed.

At last, God decided to find a new king to replace Saul.

David and Goliath

God chose a young man named David to be the new king, but there were other things God needed him to do before he took the throne. God loved David, and was always with him.

David was a shepherd. He was a great shot with a slingshot, because he used it every day to protect his father's sheep from fierce lions and bears. He was clever in other ways, too. He was famous for playing the harp, and he was summoned to the palace to play for King Saul.

"Can you soothe the king with your playing?" one of Saul's servants asked David. "He is in a terrible mood."

"Of course," answered David, and began to play. Sure enough, when the king heard David's sweet music, he quickly became calmer and happier.

Far away, King Saul's battle with the Philistines was not going well. The Philistines had a fierce warrior named Goliath on their side—he was three meters tall, and much stronger than an ox! He was very proud, too.

"Send your greatest warrior to fight me!" Goliath sneered. "If he kills me, we Philistines will be your slaves. If I kill him, you will be ours."

Only David was brave enough to take up the challenge. He knew that God would protect him.

On the day of the fight, Saul offered David his own armor and sword, but David preferred to fight without it. He picked up his slingshot, put five smooth stones in a pouch on his belt, and set off to find Goliath.

Goliath laughed when he saw David. "The Israelites' greatest fighter is a boy with a slingshot!" he said.

But David stood his ground. "I come in the name of the God of Israel," he said. "I am not afraid!"

As Goliath moved closer to attack him, David pulled one of the small stones from his pouch, put it in his slingshot, took aim, and fired. The stone hit Goliath right between the eyes, making him lose his balance and fall to the ground.

He was dead.

When the Philistine army saw this, they ran away into the hills. The Israelites had won!

Years later, after Saul died, David became the new king. His greatest wish was to conquer the city of Jerusalem, so he could keep the sacred box of God's laws there—a box containing the two stone tablets with the Ten Commandments written on them. After many years, he succeeded. He built a royal palace there and made Jerusalem God's city.

King Solomon

God loved King David and promised him that his sons would always be kings. So David told his son Solomon, "When I die, you must be a strong king, trust in God, and follow His commands. Then God will keep His promise." Solomon agreed to follow his father's advice.

In time, Solomon became king and, one night, he dreamt that God asked him, "What do you need from Me?"

Solomon replied, "I am very young to rule over so many people. Please give me wisdom to make right and true decisions."

This answer pleased God, and He gave Solomon more wisdom and understanding than anyone had ever had before.

Solomon was a good king in the beginning, and he made Israel rich and peaceful. But, over the years, he changed. He became greedy and proud, and—even worse—he did not stay faithful to God.

Solomon had to be punished. When he died, God split the kingdom of Israel in two. The northern part was ruled by a man named Jeroboam, who had once been one of Solomon's servants. The southern part, a much smaller part of the kingdom, was named Judah, and was ruled by Solomon's son, Rehoboam.

Daniel and the Lions

Over many, many years, God's people began to disobey Him. They forgot that the land they were living in was a gift from Him. So God allowed Nebuchadnezzar, the King of Babylon, to capture Jerusalem. Many Israelites died or ran away, and there was famine in the city.

Nebuchadnezzar took many prisoners from Jerusalem back to Babylon, including a group of young men from noble Israelite families. One of them was named Daniel.

Daniel was a good man who loved God, and did his best to obey Him. Even though Daniel was living in Babylon, he stayed true to God.

After some years, the Persians captured Babylon, and their leader, Darius, became king. Daniel could read and write Babylonian, and had grown very wise, so he became one of Darius's chief advisors. He served the king well—too well, perhaps, for the other advisors grew jealous and plotted against him.

Daniel prayed to God every day, and the advisors decided that this was how they would get their revenge on him. They persuaded King Darius to make a terrible new law: if a person asked any god or human being, other than the king, for anything during the next thirty days, he would be thrown into a pit of lions!

Daniel heard about the law, but kept on praying to God. His enemies were delighted—their plan had worked! They rushed to tell the king that Daniel had disobeyed him.

Darius was very sad, because he liked Daniel, but Daniel had broken the law. There was no way to save him. So, at sunset, Daniel was thrown into a pit full of hungry lions.

The king felt terrible that night. He could not rest, thinking about Daniel. As soon as dawn broke, he hurried to the lion pit. He called down into the pit, "Daniel, was your God able to save you from the lions?" He thought that Daniel must be dead, so he didn't expect an answer—but, to his amazement, he heard a voice!

"Your Majesty," said Daniel, "God knew that I was innocent and He has kept me safe. I have done you no wrong."

Daniel was freed at once, and the men who had accused him were thrown to the lions instead. Then, Darius made a new law: "Let everyone in my kingdom fear and respect the God of Daniel, for He is the one true, living God."

Jonah and the Whale

Jonah lived a simple life in a small village and kept to himself. He liked to sit in the sun outside his house and feed the birds. He didn't like to get involved in other people's problems.

But, one day, Jonah heard a voice that seemed to come from nowhere.

"Jonah, son of Amittai, you will be my prophet," it said.

Jonah jumped to his feet and looked around, but he could see no one.

Then, the voice spoke again, and Jonah knew that it was the voice of God.

"Go to the city of Nineveh and tell the people that they have been very wicked," God said. "Tell them that, if they don't change their ways, I will destroy the city."

Jonah shook with fear.

"Me?" he thought. "God wants me to leave here and go all the way to Nineveh? Who would listen to an unimportant Israelite like me?"

He didn't care about the Ninevites, their wickedness, or their city, and he thought they deserved to be punished by God. Why would God have chosen him? It must be a mistake. Jonah decided to ignore the voice. But God cannot be ignored.

"Jonah, hurry yourself," He said. "Get yourself to Nineveh!"

Jonah gathered some food and water for the journey, but he felt worried and annoyed. The same thought kept running through his mind: "I don't want to get involved in the Ninevites' problems. I just want to be left alone."

Jonah decided to run away to avoid doing God's work. So he left his home, but he did not set out for Nineveh. Instead, he headed for Joppa, a sea port, and got on a ship that was going to Tarshish.

"Maybe God won't notice that I am traveling in the wrong direction," Jonah thought. "By the time I get to Tarshish, it will be too late. I will be so far away from Nineveh that God will have to find Himself a new prophet!"

The sun beat down on Jonah's face and he started to relax. Perhaps he really could avoid God's plan for him. The ship left Joppa, and Jonah heaved a sigh of relief.

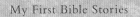

But God could read Jonah's thoughts, and He knew that His prophet was trying to escape. He made the wind blow stronger and stronger, until the ship was in the heart of a terrible storm.

The ship creaked and rocked as if it would tear apart. Terrified, the sailors threw the cargo into the sea to lighten the load, but the mighty waves just grew higher.

In his bunk, Jonah shivered, knowing that God had sent the storm because he had not done what God had told him to do. Jonah got out of his bed and staggered up to the deck. Colossal waves were breaking right across the ship, and the sailors were clinging on for dear life. When Jonah saw how frightened they were, he felt very guilty.

"This is all my fault," he shouted above the roar of the ocean. "I have made God angry. Throw me overboard and save yourselves."

At first, the captain refused to throw his passenger overboard, but the sea became wilder. Hail lashed the decks, and bitter winds tore at the sailors. Desperate to save their lives, the sailors pushed Jonah into the cold sea.

"God, help me, please!" cried Jonah as he fell.

Water closed over Jonah's head, and filled his nose and mouth. He rose to the surface, coughing and spluttering. Although he was frightened, he could see that the sea was growing calmer and the wind dying down. The hail had stopped.

"Thank goodness," said Jonah. "Whatever happens to me, the ship and all the sailors are safe."

Suddenly, Jonah felt himself being sucked into darkness.
"I'm going to drown!" he thought.

Jonah and the Whale

He stretched out his arms as he was pulled down, and felt soft, warm walls all around him. In a panic, he kicked his legs and flailed his arms, but still he was pulled further down.

At last, Jonah landed on something soft and staggered to his feet.

"Where am I?" he whispered.

Looking around, he saw a vast, dim cavern that smelled of fish. A thin spear of light was shining from above, and when Jonah looked up he saw a hole high over his head.

Then he felt the cavern move, and he realized the truth in a flash of amazement: Jonah had been swallowed by a whale!

God had seen His prophet alone and helpless in the sea. He was pleased that Jonah had sacrificed himself to save the sailors, so He had sent the whale to keep Jonah safe.

Kneeling down, Jonah spoke to God. "I am sorry for disobeying you," he said. "Please let me out of here!"

There was no reply. Jonah beat his hands against the side of the whale, but he could not escape.

Jonah lay inside the whale for three days and three nights. He was tired, wet, and cold, and he felt weak with hunger and thirst. Worst of all, he was gripped by fear. What if he were stuck inside the whale forever? What was God's plan for him?

At last, Jonah shut his eyes and prayed.

"God, I am ready," he whispered into the darkness. "I will gladly do what you asked."

Suddenly, everything started to shake, and light flooded the cavern. Jonah squeezed his eyes shut as he tumbled head over heels through the whale.

"What is happening?" he cried.

When Jonah opened his eyes, he was lying on soft, warm sand. The whale had thrown him up onto dry land. Then Jonah heard God's voice once again.

"Go to the city of Nineveh, Jonah," said God. "Do what I have asked of you."

"I will," Jonah promised.

He climbed to his feet and set off right away.

When he arrived in Nineveh, Jonah thought that no one would believe he was a prophet. But he kept his promise and preached in marketplaces. He spread God's message from slums to palaces, in temples, and in shacks.

"Turn to God and repent, or He will punish you," Jonah told the people.

To his surprise, people stopped to hear him speak. They believed what he said, and God's word spread. Even the King of Nineveh listened to Jonah's message. He changed his royal robes for clothes made of sackcloth, to show how sad he was.

"No one in Nineveh will eat or drink until we have shown God that we are sorry for all the things we have done wrong," said the king. "I hope that He will be able to forgive us."

God heard Nineveh's prayers and was pleased with Jonah.

"I will not destroy the city," He told Jonah. "They have obeyed me, so I will show mercy."

But, instead of feeling proud of having helped save the city, Jonah felt anger raging inside him. Why hadn't the Ninevites been punished?

"The Ninevites don't deserve to be forgiven!" he cried.

"Is it right for you to be angry?" asked God.

Jonah did not reply. He stormed out of the city—but soon the scorching midday sun was burning down on his head.

Jonah staggered to the side of the road and dropped to the ground under a bare tree. He was exhausted and furious, and there was no shelter from the sun.

"I wish I had never come here," he fumed. "I didn't ask to get involved."

As Jonah sat there in a rage, God made fresh, green leaves unfurl from the bare branches of the tree. The tree grew larger and curved itself over Jonah, until he was lying in its shade. As his body cooled down, his temper cooled, too.

"Thank you, God," he murmured as he drifted off to sleep.

At sunrise, God sent a worm to eat Jonah's tree. Its leaves shriveled up and fell from the branches. Jonah awoke to find the sun blazing down on him again.

"Why did you kill the tree, God?" Jonah raged. "It was a good tree and provided me with shelter."

"You are angry because the tree did not deserve to die," God said. "How would I have felt if I'd had to let Nineveh burn? If the tree deserves a second chance, surely my people deserve a second chance, too? And what about you, and the whale who saved you?"

Jonah bowed his head in shame. Now, he could see what God was trying to show him.

"I'm sorry," he whispered.

God had saved the people of Nineveh, just as He had sent the whale to save Jonah, because God loves all His people.

The Christmas Story

Long ago, in a place called Nazareth, there lived a young woman named Mary. She was engaged to be married to Joseph, a carpenter, and loved to daydream about their future life together.

One day, as she swept her yard, Mary noticed a stranger
smiling at her. She didn't know who he was, and she
was frightened.

"My name is Gabriel," the stranger said. "I have brought
you a message from God."

Mary was too amazed to speak.

"Don't be afraid," said Gabriel. "God has chosen you to
do something special for Him. Soon, you will have a baby.
He will be God's own son and he will be king. You are to call
him Jesus."

Mary trusted God, so she agreed to do what He asked of her. But Joseph felt upset, because he knew he wasn't the father of the baby.

"I love Mary, but I don't know if I should still marry her," he thought. So he prayed to God for help.

God heard his prayers and, that night, He sent an angel to visit Joseph in a dream.

The angel was gentle and kind.

"Do not worry, Joseph," he said. "You should marry Mary and love her as your wife. She is the most special of women, chosen by God to be the mother of His son. The baby will be named Jesus, which means 'savior,' because he will save his people."

When Joseph woke up, he decided to marry Mary right away.

"I trust in God," he said to himself.

So Mary and Joseph were married, and they waited patiently for the baby to arrive.

Soon after the wedding, Emperor Augustus, who ruled over the land where Mary and Joseph lived, decided to make a list of all the people in his empire to make sure they paid their taxes. He sent out orders through his messengers to every town and city in the land.

"Everyone must travel back to the place they were born to be counted," said the messengers.

Joseph had been born in Bethlehem, far away from Nazareth.

"My wife can't travel now—she's going to have a baby soon," Joseph said to the messenger. "She should stay home in comfort, not travel far away. Can we go to Bethlehem another time?"

The messenger shook his head.

"No," he said sternly. "This is the Emperor's order. You must go now."

The journey to Bethlehem took many days. The roads were bone-dry and dusty, and the sun beat down. Often, Mary had to stop and rest.

At last, late one night, they arrived in Bethlehem. Joseph looked at Mary and saw how tired she was.

"We'll find a place to stay for the night," he reassured her. But Bethlehem was packed with people who had followed the Emperor's orders, and every inn they tried was full.

They reached the very last inn in town, but the innkeeper
said, "There is no room. You'll have to try somewhere else."
"What can we do?" pleaded Mary. "My baby is coming soon."
The innkeeper was a kind man and saw how tired Mary was.
"Come with me," he said. "I have a place that might do."

NO
ROOM

The innkeeper led them to a barn behind the inn.

"I know it's not much," said the innkeeper, "but it's warm and dry."

Mary and Joseph looked inside. The barn was filled with animals and the floor was covered with fresh hay.

"My baby will be safe here," said Mary. "Thank you for your kindness."

Later that night, Mary gave birth to a little boy, the Son of God, just as the angel had said. Joseph lined the manger with fresh hay to make a soft bed. Mary wrapped the baby in a blanket and laid him down gently.

"We will love you and care for you, little one, and we will call you Jesus," whispered Mary.

High on a hillside nearby, some shepherds were looking after their sheep. The night was dark and still, and the sheep were dozing peacefully.

Suddenly, there was a dazzling brightness in the sky and an angel appeared.

"What's happening?" cried the shepherds, huddling together in fear.

"Do not be afraid," said the angel. "I have the most wonderful news for you and for all the people on Earth. The Son of God has been born in Bethlehem. He is the king who will save humankind, just as God promised."

More angels appeared and sang, "Glory to God, and peace to everyone on Earth!"

Then, suddenly, the angels were gone. The shepherds looked at each other in wonder.

"Can it be true?" said one shepherd to another.

"Without a doubt," the second shepherd replied. "We must go to Bethlehem and see the baby at once."

NO ROOM

NO ROOM

The shepherds ran down from the hillside and through the dark streets of Bethlehem. They ran and ran, until at last they heard a baby's cry and found the barn where Jesus was sleeping.

"We have come to see the new king," they told Joseph excitedly. "God sent an angel to tell us about him."

"You are all welcome," said Joseph.

So the shepherds went inside and saw Mary with the tiny baby in the manger.

"Wonderful!" said the first shepherd.

"Our savior!" said the second, as they kneeled to gaze at him.

"We are poor. We have no gift for him," they said to Mary. "All we have to give him is our love."

"That is the very best gift in the world," said Mary.

Soon, it was time for the shepherds to return to their sheep. They were so excited that they told everyone they met about the new king.

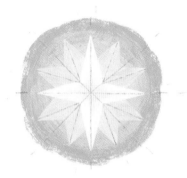

That same night, a new star appeared in the sky. In a far-off land, three wise men looked up and saw it. They knew it meant that something very special had happened.

"The star must be a sign from God. It is shining because a new king has been born, just as He promised years ago," said the first. "We must go at once and worship him."

"Perhaps the star will lead us to the baby," said the second.

"Let's take him the most special gifts," said the third. "Gifts fit for a king."

Without delay, the wise men packed their bags, climbed on their camels, and rode off toward the city of Jerusalem. They were sure they would find the new king there, at the palace.

"Where else would a king be, but in the finest of palaces?" they said to each other.

The wise men traveled across many deserts for many nights, until they finally arrived at Jerusalem. They went to the palace and asked the guards to take them to the ruler, King Herod.

"Where is the new king?" they asked him. "We have traveled far, following the new star that appeared on the night of his birth."

King Herod was shocked. He was the only king in this land, and that was how he wanted it to stay.

"Who is this new king they speak of?" he whispered to his advisor.

"A prophet once said that, one day, a new king would be born in Bethlehem," said the advisor.

"This must not be," Herod thought to himself.

"I want to worship him, too," Herod lied to the wise men. "Go to Bethlehem, then come back and tell me where he is."

Herod planned to stop the baby from taking his throne.

The wise men set off again into the night, and traveled to Bethlehem, where the star led them to Mary, Joseph, and Jesus.

"We have come to see the new king," they said to Joseph.

"You are most welcome," said Joseph.

The wise men stepped inside and saw Mary with her tiny baby, the Son of God. Quietly, the wise men kneeled down to give the baby their gifts.

"Here is precious gold," said the first.

"I have brought sweet-smelling frankincense," said the second.

"And this is myrrh, a healing oil," said the third.

"You will be a great king, a teacher, a leader, and you will save all the people of the Earth," they said to Jesus together.

Then, the wise men said goodbye and found a place to rest before starting their journey home.

While the wise men slept, God visited each of them in a dream. He warned them not to return to Herod. So, in the morning, the wise men went straight home and did not return to Jerusalem.

When King Herod learned that the wise men had disobeyed him, he was furious.

"I am the only king!" he roared. "I will not let a baby take my throne!"

Jesus was not safe in Bethlehem now, so God sent
an angel to visit Joseph while he slept.

"You must wake up!" the angel said to Joseph.
"Escape to Egypt, where you will be safe. Stay there
until I tell you to come back."

Joseph woke Mary, and they quickly loaded their
belongings onto a donkey. Then, with Mary carrying
Jesus tightly in her arms, they set off into the night.

Jesus was safe in Egypt, and he lived there peacefully with Mary and Joseph for some years. His parents missed their home in Nazareth, but, while King Herod was alive, they knew they could never return.

Then, one day, Herod died and Joseph had a dream. An angel appeared to him and said, "Joseph, it is safe for you to return home."

Joseph and Mary were overjoyed. They packed up all their belongings and set off once more, with Jesus by their side.

When they arrived, they were glad to be back in their home town at last.

Joseph held Jesus as he stood in the doorway of their little house.

"This is Nazareth, the town where you will grow up," he said with a smile. "Welcome home, Jesus!"

Jesus Visits the Temple

When Jesus was twelve years old, Mary and Joseph took him to Jerusalem for the Festival of Passover. The celebrations lasted a whole week.

After the festival, everyone began the long journey back to Nazareth. Mary and Joseph were walking with many other people, and at the end of the day they realized that they hadn't seen Jesus for a long while. They searched for him, but he was nowhere to be seen, so they hurried back to Jerusalem, hoping to find him there.

It was three days before they found Jesus—he was in the temple, listening calmly to the men who taught God's laws, and asking questions. Everyone was amazed at how much of the teaching he understood!

"We have been searching everywhere for you," said Mary. "We have been so worried. How could you do this to us?"

Jesus was surprised. "I'm sorry you were worried," he said, "but I felt so at home here in my Father's house, I stayed here."

Mary and Joseph were pleased that he was safe, and they set off again for Nazareth, with Jesus walking beside them all the way.

Jesus Is Baptized

Just before Jesus was born, Mary's cousin Elizabeth had given birth to a son named John. When John grew up, God spoke to him and said, "You will be My messenger. You will preach My word to the people."

John did so, and people traveled from far and wide to hear him speak.

"God's king is coming soon," he told them. "Tell God that you are sorry for your sins. Change your ways, then He will forgive you."

Many people were sorry for their sins, so John led them to the River Jordan and dipped their heads under the water. This was a sign that their sins had been washed away. It was called "baptism."

"Are you God's promised king?" people asked him.

"No," said John. "I am only a messenger. Someone much greater than me is coming soon."

One day, Jesus came to John and said, "Will you baptize me, too?"

They had never met before, but John knew at once that this was Jesus, God's promised king.

"You should baptize me, Lord," he said, falling to his knees.

"No, John," said Jesus. "I want the people to see me baptized and to know that it is important."

So John did as Jesus asked, and God was pleased.

Jesus and His Disciples

One morning, as Jesus walked beside Lake Galilee, he saw two fishermen pulling their fishing boats up onto the beach nearby.

"Will you take me out onto the lake?" Jesus asked them.

One of them, whose name was Simon, agreed, and Jesus began to teach from the boat. People stopped to listen along the shore.

When Jesus had finished teaching, he told Simon to row further out and drop the fishing nets there.

"We didn't catch any fish there all last night," said Simon, "but we will do as you ask."

So Simon and his brother Andrew rowed out into the middle of the lake and dropped their nets. Instantly, the nets were teeming with wriggling fish. There were so many that Simon thought the boat might sink.

"James! John!" he called to two more fishermen nearby. "We need help!"

All four fishermen were amazed to see all the fish. They knew that they were watching something very special.

Then, Jesus said to them, "Come and follow me. From now on, you will work with people, not fish."

After this, Jesus called other people to follow him, too. Altogether, he chose twelve men to be his closest companions and share his work. They were called his "disciples."

Jesus Feeds 5,000 People

As time passed, more and more people came to listen to Jesus. He would speak to the crowds for hours at a time. One day, Jesus was teaching by Lake Galilee. The day wore on and, by sunset, 5,000 people or more were gathered around him. It had been a long day, and they were all very hungry.

"Please send the people away," the disciples begged Jesus. "Tell them to walk to the farms and villages to find food."

But Jesus replied, "Why don't you give them food?"
Jesus's disciple Andrew stepped forward.

"This boy is offering five loaves and two fish, but that won't be enough to feed this crowd!" he said.

Jesus took the loaves and fish, and thanked God for them. Then, he gave the food to the disciples, who broke it up and handed it out to the people. Everyone ate as much as they wanted and, when they had finished, the disciples gathered up twelve full baskets of leftover food. It was a miracle!

Jesus Walks on Water

After this wonderful meal, Jesus told his disciples to climb into their boat and go to the other side of the lake, while he said goodbye to the crowd. Then, he went into the hills to pray.

Later that night, as the wind got stronger, the disciples in the boat saw someone walking toward them over the water.

They were terrified. "It's a ghost!" they cried.

But Jesus called to them, "Don't be afraid. It is me."

Peter said, "If this is really you, Lord, tell me to come to you over the water."

"Come, Peter," said Jesus.

So Peter got out of the boat and walked toward Jesus over the water. He watched Jesus at first, but when he noticed the waves and the wind, he became afraid and began to sink. "Save me, Lord!" he cried.

Immediately, Jesus reached out his hand to Peter and caught hold of him. "How little faith you have," he said. "Why did you doubt me? Let's get back to the boat."

As they did so, the wind stopped and the water was calm. Everyone in the boat was amazed and said to each other, "This must truly be God's son."

The Easter Story

I t was a very exciting day in Jerusalem. Riding on a humble donkey, Jesus had arrived in the city for the Festival of Passover. Cheers rang out from the crowd and palm leaves waved in the air. Everyone had come to see their king entering the city.

"God bless the king who comes in the name of the Lord!" they shouted.

Many people laid palm leaves down for the donkey to walk upon. Everyone wanted to show their love and respect.

Jesus went straight to the city's temple, where he got a terrible shock. In the temple's courtyard, people were buying goods, changing money, and selling animals. It was noisy and smelly. The air was filled with the shouts of sellers and the cries of animals. Jesus felt anger rise up inside him.

"The house of God is a house of prayer," he roared. "But you have turned it into a den of greed!"

He turned over the tables of goods, and coins rained down to the ground. The sellers scurried away, making room for people to pray. Jesus's supporters cheered, but the chief priests were furious.

"He wants to destroy our power over the people," they snarled.

The priests controlled people by making them afraid, but people listened to Jesus because he talked about love.

"If only we could get rid of him," the priests muttered.

Six days before the Festival of Passover, Jesus and his
disciples went to stay with some friends. They were served
a special meal and, while they relaxed around the table, a
woman opened a jar of expensive perfumed oil. She kneeled
down and rubbed the oil onto Jesus's feet.

"You could have sold that and given the money to the
poor," snapped Judas, one of Jesus's disciples.

"Leave her alone," said Jesus. "She is being kind."

But Judas felt angry with Jesus, and his anger allowed evil to creep into his heart. He knew that the chief priests didn't like Jesus, and he decided to help them get rid of him. Two days before Passover, he met with them and agreed to lead them to Jesus when Jesus was alone.

"I will kiss Jesus to show the guards who to arrest," he told the priests.

In return, the priests promised to pay Judas thirty pieces of silver.

Jesus knew that the priests were plotting against him. He also knew that it was all part of God's plan, and that he would leave the world soon to join his Father in heaven. But he still felt sad when he thought about what was going to happen.

The evening before Passover, Jesus took some water and kneeled in front of each of the twelve disciples in turn. He gently washed their feet and dried them on a towel.

"Lord, you should not wash our feet," said the disciples. "You are too important."

"No one is more important than anyone else," Jesus said. "Even though I am your teacher, we are all equal, because we are all God's children."

On the day of Passover, Jesus and his disciples sat down to eat a special meal together.

"Soon, one of you will betray me," Jesus told them. The disciples were shocked—all except Judas.

"Who is it?" they asked. They didn't notice Judas turning pale.

But Jesus would not speak Judas's name. He blessed the bread by saying a prayer, then broke it into pieces and handed it to his disciples.

"Like this bread, my body will be broken," he said. "Please eat it."

He blessed the wine and passed around the cup, so they could all drink from it, to show they were part of God's family.

"This wine is like my blood, which will be spilled for many people," he said. "Please drink it."

As they ate and drank, Jesus watched his disciples with sadness in his heart.

"Eat and drink to remember me," he said. "We won't have another meal together until we are in God's kingdom."

There was a quiet garden called Gethsemane, where Jesus liked to pray. After the meal, he took Peter, James, and John there to pray with him. While they rested, Jesus fell to his knees to pray. He knew that the priests were coming for him, and he felt afraid.

"Father, I know what needs to happen, but it's going to be very hard," he said. "Please help me."

Jesus spoke to God for a long time and his disciples fell asleep.

Soon, Judas entered the garden. Judas was followed by men armed with swords and fiery torches.

"Rise!" Jesus called. "Here comes the traitor."

Peter, James, and John rose quickly, but it was too late. Judas walked up to Jesus and kissed his cheek. It was his signal to the guards that this was the man to arrest. The guards grabbed Jesus by the arms and held him tightly. Peter wanted to fight, but Jesus stopped him.

"My Father in heaven will protect me," he said.

The chief priests took Jesus to Pontius Pilate, the Roman governor. The Romans were in charge of Jerusalem, so it was Pilate's job to decide what would happen to prisoners.

Pilate questioned Jesus, trying to find out if Jesus was an enemy of Rome. He knew that the chief priests wanted Jesus dead, but he believed Jesus was harmless.

Early the next morning, a large crowd had gathered.

"Do you want me to release the King of the Jews?" Pilate asked them.

The chief priests had already talked to the crowd and told them lies about Jesus.

"No!" the people shouted. "Crucify him!"

"Why?" Pilate asked. "What crime has he committed?"

But the crowd just kept shouting, "Crucify him!"

Pilate was a weak man and he wanted to please the people. So he had Jesus beaten and then handed him over to be crucified.

The soldiers dressed Jesus in a purple robe to make fun of him. Purple was the color that kings wore, and they thought he had been pretending to be a king. They wanted to mock him and laugh at him. They even twisted together some thorns to make a crown.

"Hail, King of the Jews!" they shouted, laughing at him.

Jesus was forced to carry a heavy, wooden cross through the crowded city streets. All the way, people jeered and shouted at him. It was very different from the way he had arrived in Jerusalem.

At nine o'clock in the morning, the soldiers nailed Jesus to the cross.

"Father, forgive them," Jesus whispered. "They don't understand what they are doing."

The minutes crept by like hours and Jesus was in great pain. It became harder and harder for him to breathe. A crowd gathered, shouting nasty things at Jesus and making fun of him.

"If you were really the Son of God, you would save yourself," they jeered. "Come down from the cross!"

Jesus did not reply. He felt as if each breath was tearing at his body. The sun shrank away, and the sky became dark and stormy, but the crowd and the priests kept shouting their cruel words.

Finally, at three o'clock, with a loud cry, the Son of God took his last breath.

Later that day, a Roman named Joseph took down Jesus's body, wrapped it in linen, and placed it in a tomb. Then, he rolled a large, heavy stone over the entrance.

Early the next morning, Mary Magdalene, one of Jesus's friends, came to visit the tomb. To her amazement, she found that the large stone had been rolled away.

Mary stepped into the dark tomb and saw that Jesus's body was gone. All that was left were the strips of linen in which he had been wrapped.

"He is not here," said a voice.

Mary turned and saw a man dressed all in white. He was an angel, but she did not know that. She gasped in fear.

"Do not be afraid," the man said. "Jesus has risen! Go, tell his disciples."

Trembling with shock and overcome with happiness, Mary fled from the tomb and ran to find Peter and John.

At first, Peter and John did not believe Mary's story. They followed her to the tomb and ran inside.

"Someone has stolen the body!" they cried. "Who could have done such a thing?"

They went to tell the other disciples what had happened, but Mary stayed behind.

"What shall I do?" she cried, tears running down her face.

She was afraid to be there alone, but she did not want to go home, either.

"Mary," said a familiar voice.

She knew Jesus's voice at once. But how could it be him? A man stepped forward.

"Master!" Mary cried, falling to her knees before him.

"Tell the disciples what you have seen," said Jesus. "I will soon be with my Father in heaven."

Mary ran back to find the disciples.

"I have seen my Lord with my own eyes," she cried. "He has risen from the grave!"

Over the next forty days, Jesus appeared many times to his disciples. On the Mount of Olives, near Jerusalem, he spoke to them one last time.

"It is time for me to return to my Father in heaven," he said. "Everything has happened just as He said it would. But I will always be with you."

The sun burst out from behind a bank of clouds. As golden beams of light dazzled them, the disciples watched Jesus rise up to heaven. Then, two angels appeared, dressed in shimmering white.

"Jesus will come back to you," they promised.

The disciples shared smiles of love and happiness. They knew that, until Jesus returned, they would keep his words alive. They would spread his message of love throughout the world.